Exotic Guitar Scales
Arpeggios and Modes from Around the World

John Wallace

Copyright
John Wallace
Exotic Guitar Scales: Arpeggios and Modes from Around the World

© 2014, John Wallace Music
http://www.exoticguitarresources.com

Cover artwork & design ©2014 George Coghill
http://georgecoghill.com

ALL RIGHTS RESERVED. This book contains material protected under International and Federal Copyright Laws and Treaties. Any unauthorized reprint or use of this material is prohibited. No part of this book may be reproduced or transmitted in any form or by any means, electronic or mechanical, including photocopying, recording, or by any information storage and retrieval system without express written permission from the author / publisher.

Acknowledgements

I'd like to thank the following people: Warren Henry and Jeffrey Imel for opening the door of improvisational music to me, my uncle Chuck Cooper for inspiring me to play, George Coghill for motivating me to write this and for contributing the awesome art work for the cover, and to my wife, Michelle, for her support and editorial contributions.

I would also like to thank the countless musicians and teachers who over the years and across the miles have inspired me, taught me, and created music with me, whose community support helped shape the musician that I am.

Contents

Introduction	5
C Diminished Scale	10
C Diminished Scale Positions	12
C Diminished Arpeggios	13
C Double Harmonic Scale (Arabic or Byzantine Scale)	16
C Double Harmonic Scale Positions	17
C Double Harmonic Arpeggios	18
C Harmonic Minor Scale	19
C Harmonic Minor Scale Positions	20
C Harmonic Minor Arpeggios	21
C Hungarian Gypsy Scale	22
C Hungarian Gypsy Scale Positions	23
C Hungarian Gypsy Arpeggios	24
C Japanese (Sakura) Scale	25
C Japanese (Sakura) Scale Positions	26
C Japanese (Sakura) Arpeggios	27
C Neapolitan Major Scale	28
C Neapolitan Major Scale Positions	29
C Neapolitan Major Arpeggios	30
C Neapolitan Minor Scale	31
C Neapolitan Minor Scale Positions	32
C Neapolitan Minor Arpeggios	33
C Persian Scale	34
C Persian Scale Positions	35
C Persian Scale Arpeggios	36
C Prometheus Scale	37
C Prometheus Scale Positions	38
C Prometheus Scale Arpeggios	39

Introduction

I wrote this book to share some of the information I've learned over the years from studying exotic scales for guitar. Like you, I wondered how guitarists such as John Mclaughlin, Al Di Meola, Paco De Lucia, and more recently Rodrigo y Gabriela, created such an exotic feel in their music, and I wanted to know how I could incorporate those sounds into my own repertoire. Once I discovered they were not always playing in the standard modes, I set out to learn everything I could about scales from around the world.

My journey took me on a 10+ years long quest, studying jazz in Cuba with legends such as Jorge Chicoy, Bobby Carcasses and Norberto Rodriguez and flamenco from guitarists across the United States. I studied classical guitar with George Bachmann at Kent State University and Stephen Aron at the University of Akron, and I studied jazz guitar with Warren Henry, Jeffrey Imel, Bob Ferrazza, and Jack Zucker, to name just a few.

In this book, I've distilled the essence of the most useful of all this research in a concise, easy-to-learn format. In "Exotic Guitar Scales", you will learn the scale, scale construction, harmonies, scale positions and arpeggios for some of the best exotic scales out there, adding a richness to your playing and extending the sonic palette from which you can express yourself.

For each of the scales, I've written out the scale position in an easy-to-understand, common format. For example, the following scale shows the first position of the Persian scale in a fretboard diagram that guitarists will already be familiar with:

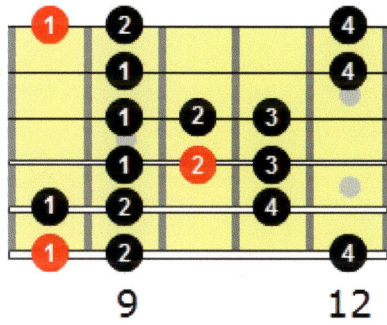

Each of the dots represents a note on the fretboard, and the numbers in the dots represent the left hand fingering to be used. The notes should be read from left to right, bottom to top, as the lowest E string runs along the bottom of the fretboard, and the highest at the top:

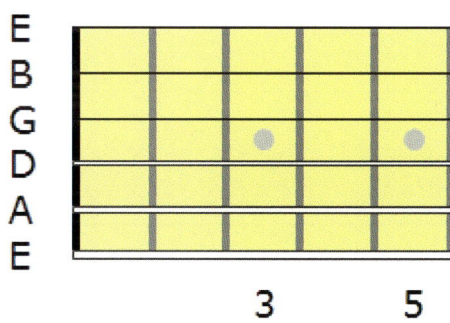

In addition to the scales, I've also written out the root position of the arpeggios listed for each of these scales. Though the arpeggios are written out in the root position, you can use the notes to explore the rest of the inversions for each arpeggio. For example, if the book lists a C7b5 arpeggio:

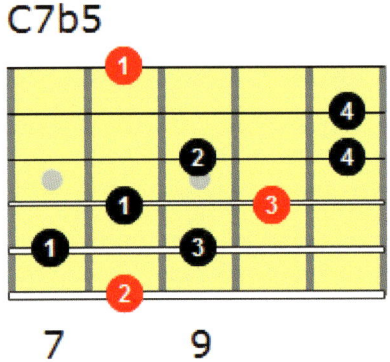

You can find the rest of the inversions like:

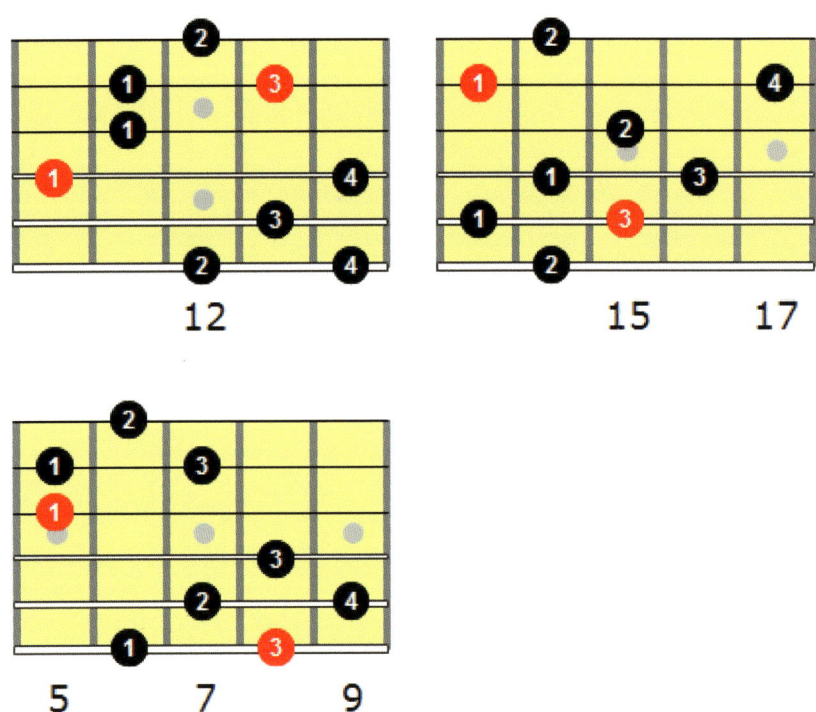

It's also a good exercise to limit the arpeggios to just certain string groups and find the inversions on that string group. An example of this would be the following diagrams detailing a CMaj7b5 arpeggio played only on the G, B and high E strings:

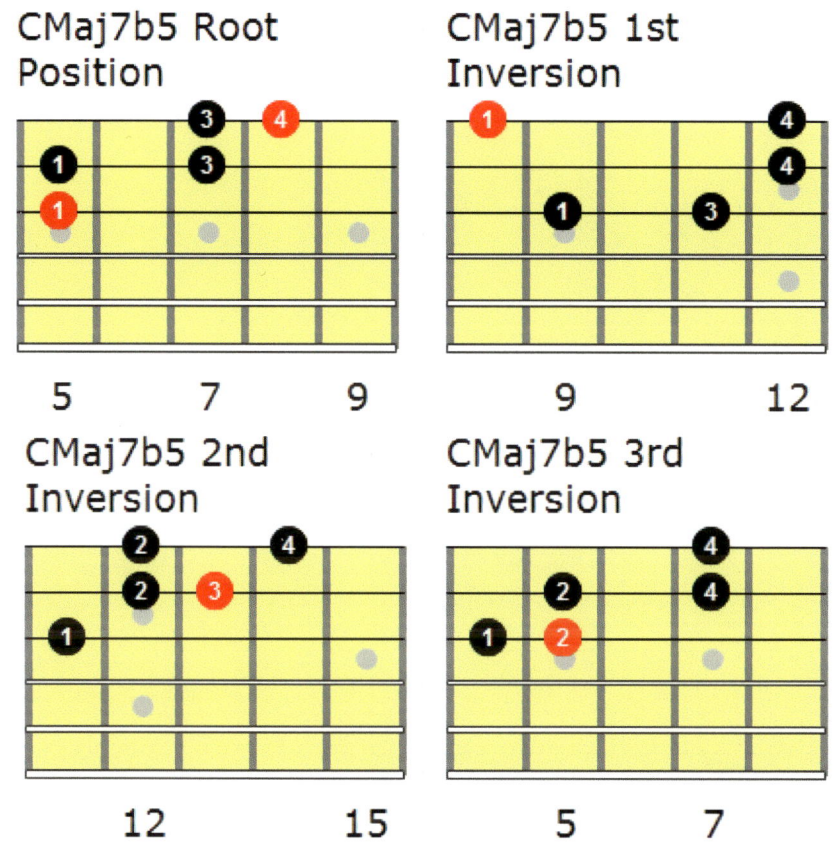

Furthermore, you can find all the 4-note, one-octave arpeggios in a given scale position. For example, in the C Prometheus scale you might find these arpeggios:

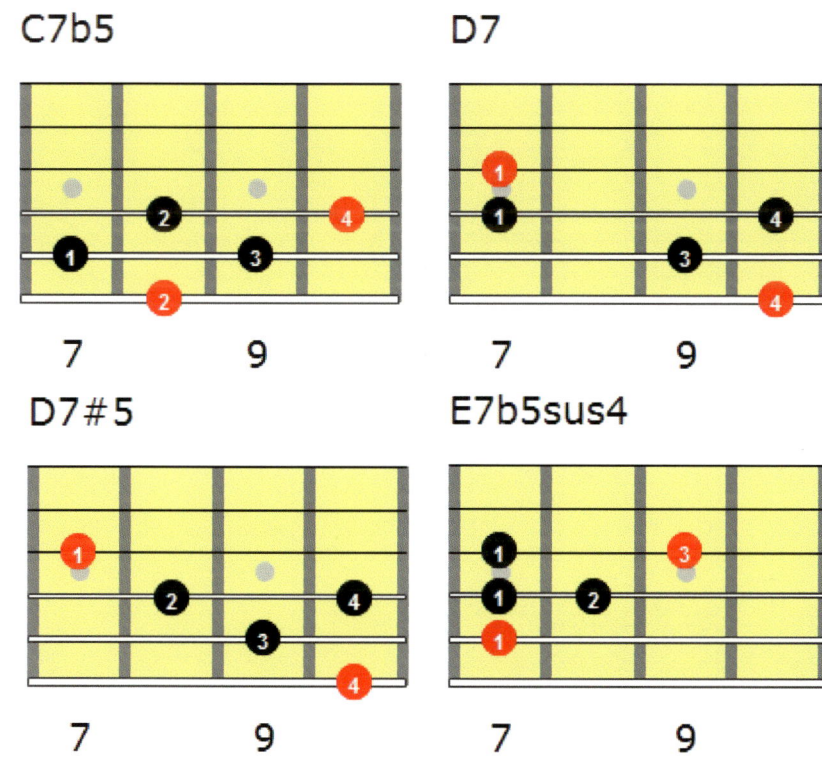

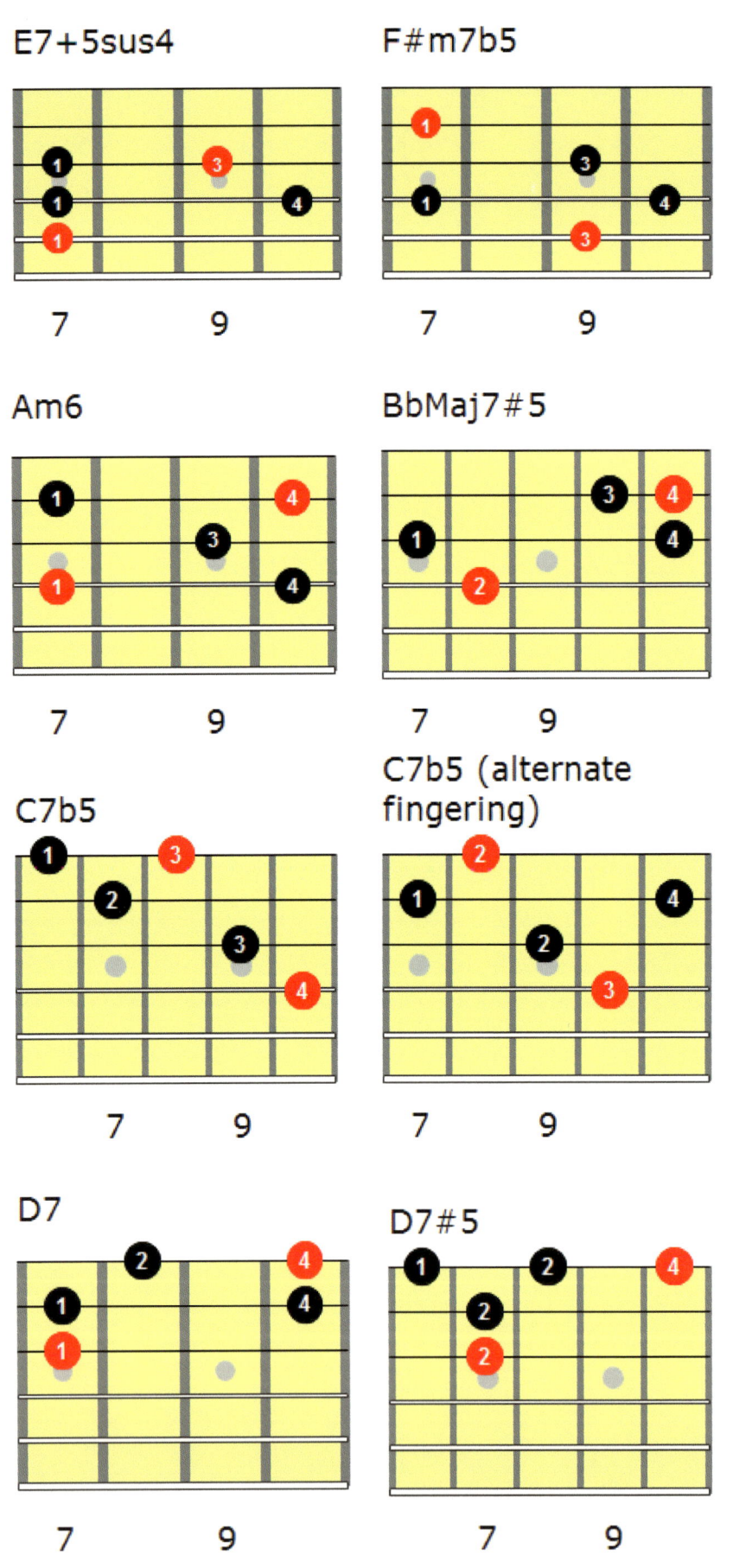

A few notes about the examples in this book:
- For brevity's sake, all scales are written out with the root being C.
- Root notes for the scales and arpeggios are listed in the red dots.
- Enharmonic equivalents are written as Eb(D#) where it seemed important to identify the enharmonic equivalent.
- The numbers in the neck diagrams are meant to indicate left hand fingerings.
- The fingerings I've written out for the scales are the fingerings I'm most comfortable with. However, if you find that changing some of the fingerings helps you get the scales and arpeggios under your hands, you should do that.
- I chose the arpeggios I thought were most interesting from these scales and named them in a way that I thought best described their character. There are certainly many more arpeggios to be discovered in these scales than what are listed here.
  - Most of the time, I've written the arpeggios to their highest root note in a given position, while in others, I extended the form to include the 3rd above that to show that the arpeggios can be extended beyond the last root note in a given position.

This book gives a good overview of exotic scales that can lend a very unique sound to your playing. It's my hope that this book will give you a solid foundation for exploring scales and modes from around the world--information you need to take your guitar playing to the next level. There are more exotic scales to be discovered out there, and once you master what's in this book you will have the skills you need to explore other modes on your own!

I hope you enjoy the following material. Please visit http://www.exoticguitarresources.com for audio, video and more musical examples.

C Diminished Scale

Scale Notes:

C - Db – Eb – E – F#(Gb) - G – A – Bb - C

Scale Intervals:

h W h W h W h W

Chords/Arpeggios:

Chord	Spelling
Cdim7	C – Eb – F#(Gb) - A
C7	C – E – G – Bb
C7b5	C – E – F#(Gb) – Bb
Cmin7	C – Eb – G – Bb
Cmin7b5	C – Eb – F#(Gb) - Bb
Dbdim7	Db – E(Fb) – G - Bb
Ebdim7	Eb – F#(Gb) – A - C
Eb7	Eb – G – Bb – Db
Eb7b5	Eb – G – A(Bbb) – Db
Ebmin7	Eb – F#(Gb) – Bb – Db
Ebmin7b5	Eb – F#(Gb) – A(Bbb) - Db
Edim7	E – G – Bb - Db
F#dim7	F# - A – C - Eb
F#7	F# - Bb(A#) – Db(C#) - E
F#7b5	F# - Bb(A#) – C - E

F#min7	F# - A – Db(C#) – E
F#min7b5	F# - A – C - E
Gdim7	G – Bb – Db - E
Adim7	A – C – Eb – F#(Gb)
A7	A – Db(C#) – E – G
A7b5	A – Db(C#) – Eb - G
Amin7	A – C – E – G
Amin7b5	A – C – Eb – G
Bbdim7	Bb – Db – E - G

C Diminished Scale Positions

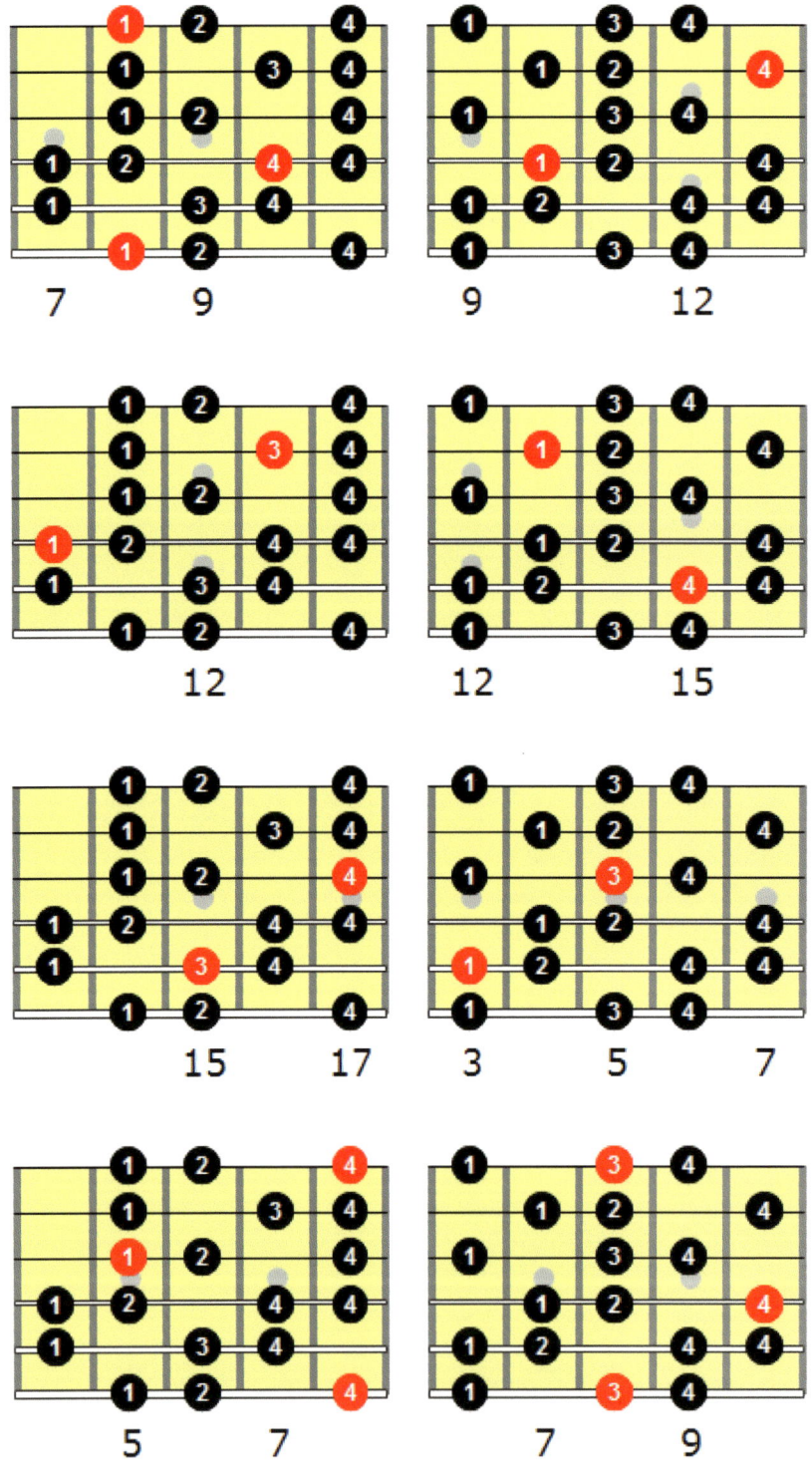

C Diminished Arpeggios

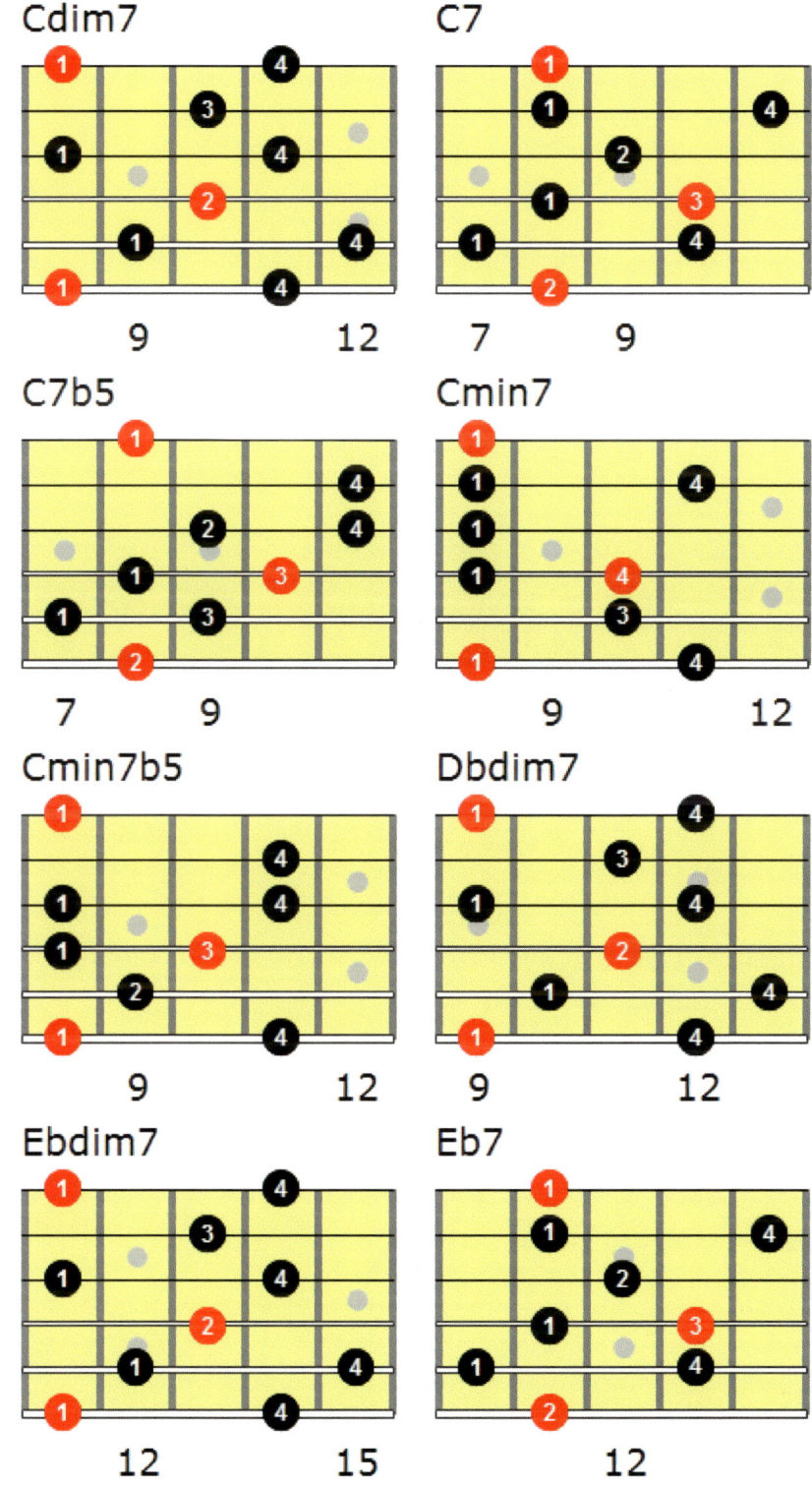

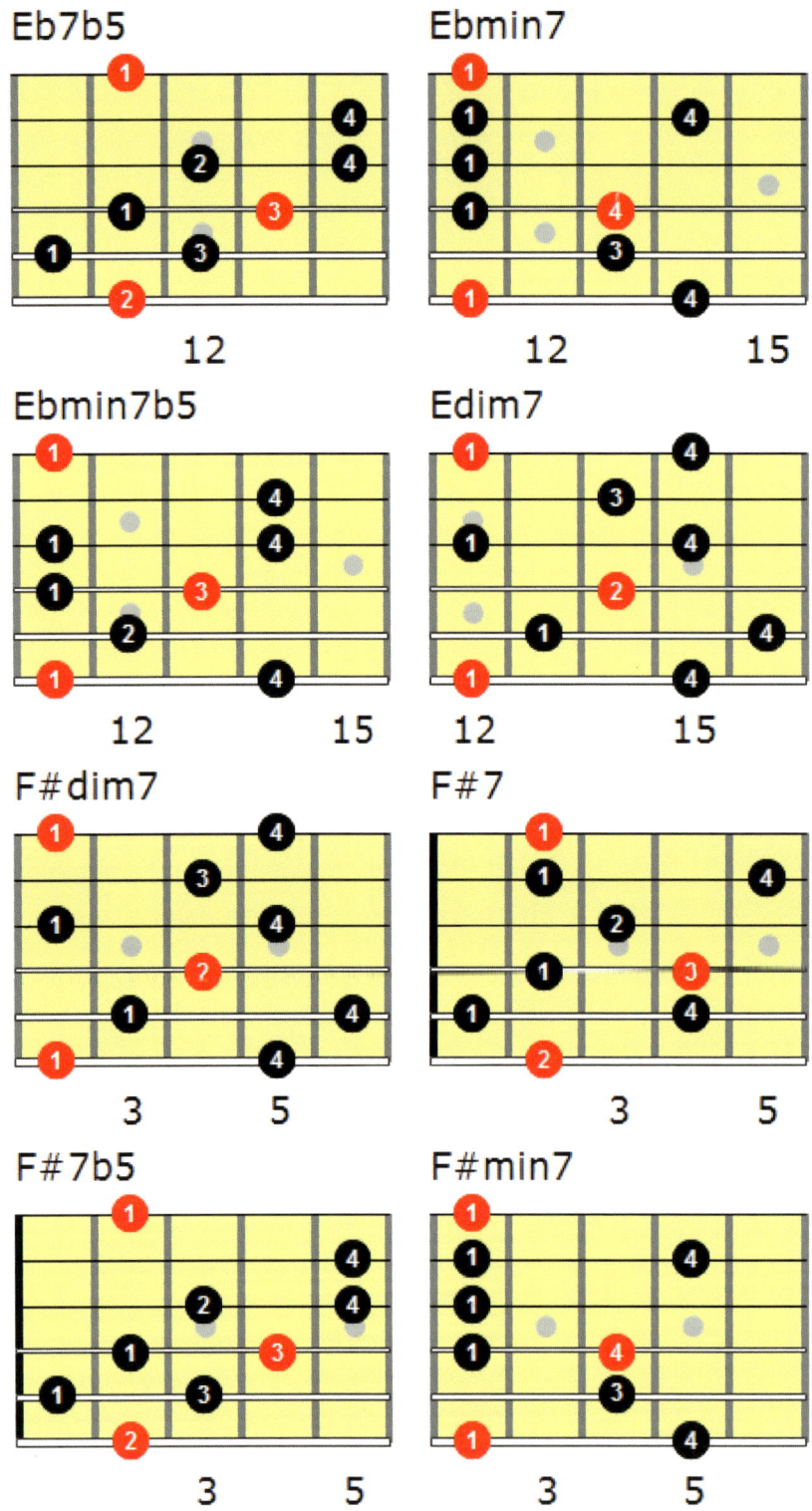

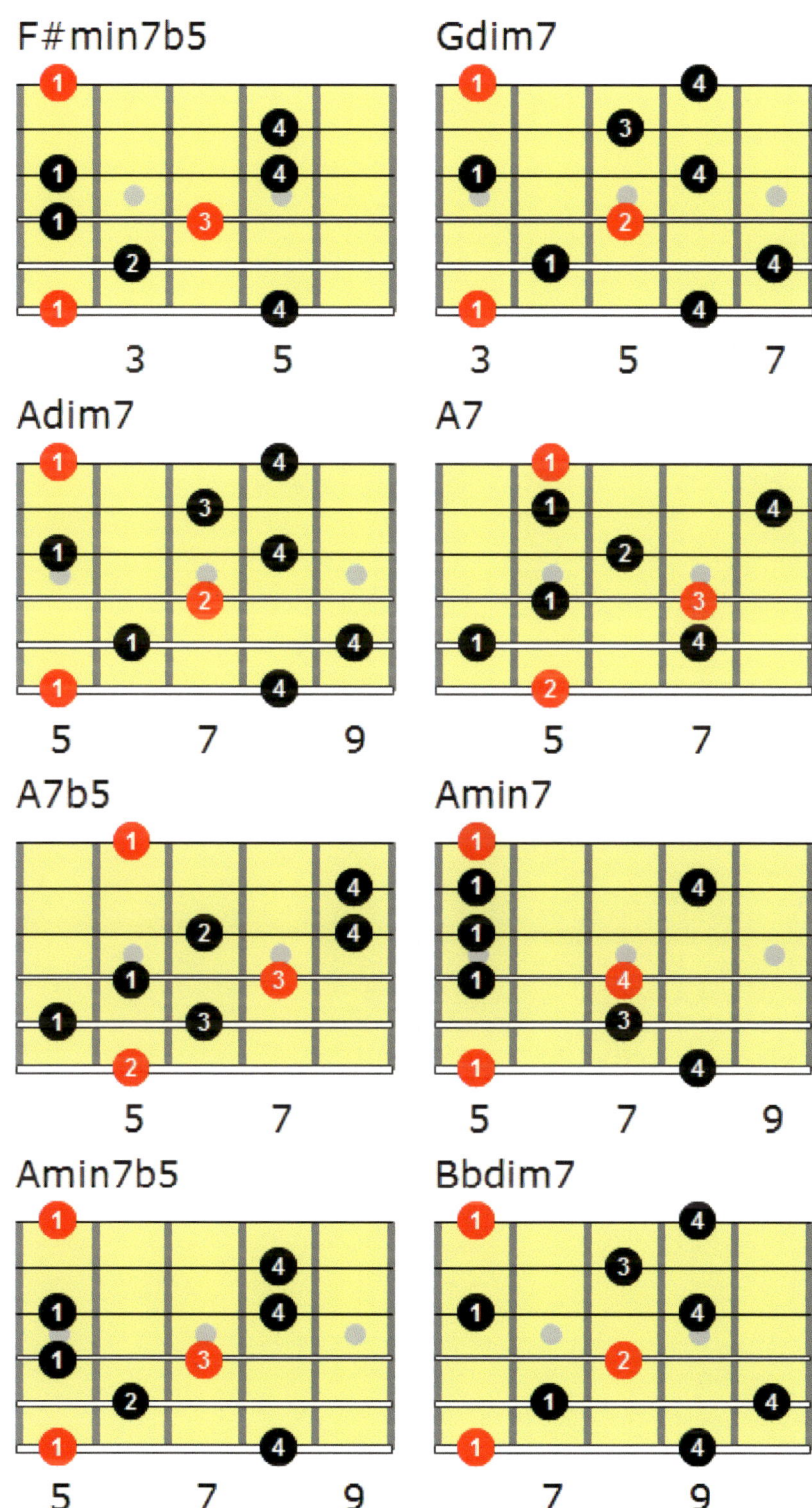

C Double Harmonic Scale (Arabic or Byzantine Scale)

Scale Notes:

C - Db - E - F - G - Ab - B - C

Scale Intervals:

h (W+h) h W h (W+h) h

Chords/Arpeggios:

Chord	Spelling
CMaj7	C - E - G - B
Db7	Db - F - Ab – B(Cb)
Em6	E - G - B - Db (C#)
Fmin/Maj7	F - Ab - C - E
G7b5	G - B - Db - F
AbMaj7#5	Ab - C - E - G
Bdim7sus4	B - E - F - Ab

C Double Harmonic Scale Positions

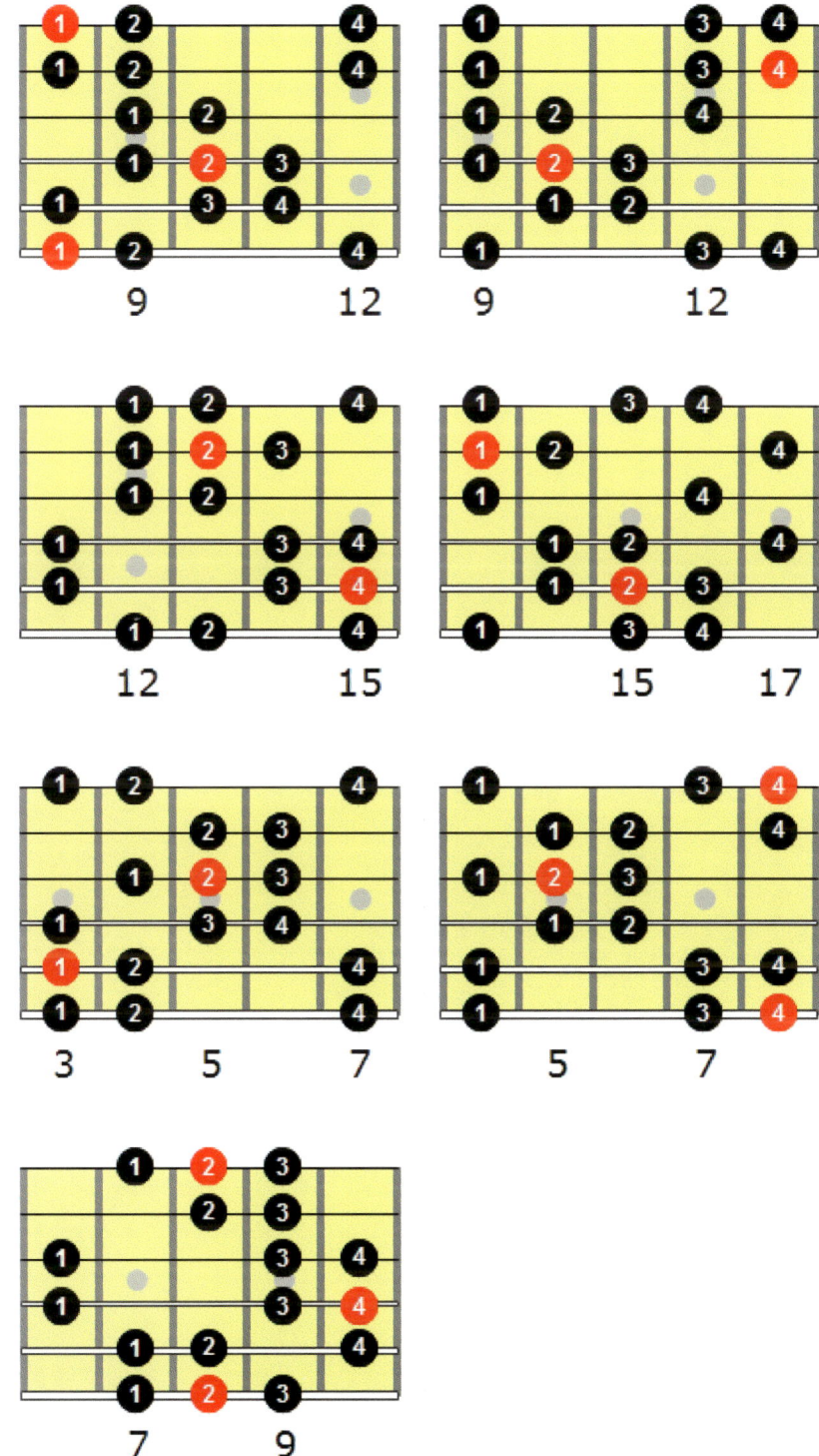

C Double Harmonic Arpeggios

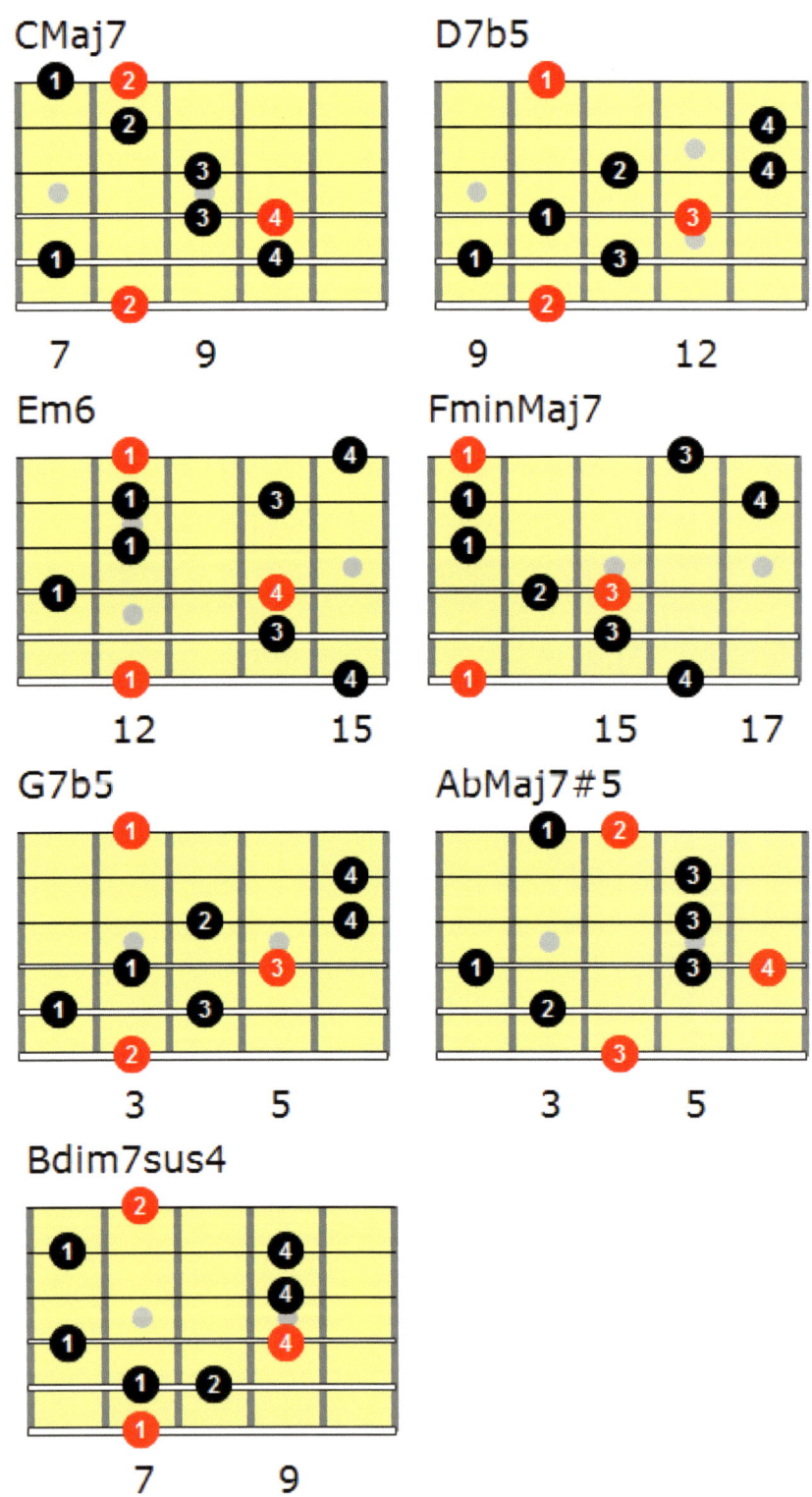

C Harmonic Minor Scale

Scale Notes:

C – D – Eb – F – G – Ab – B - C

Scale Intervals:

W h W W h (W+h) h

Chords/Arpeggios:

Chord	Spelling
CminMaj7	C – Eb – G – B
Dmin7b5	D – F – Ab – C
EbMaj7#5	Eb – G - B - D
Fm7	F – Ab – C – Eb
G7	G – B – D – F
AbMaj7	Ab – C – Eb – G
Bdim7	B – D – F - Ab

C Harmonic Minor Scale Positions

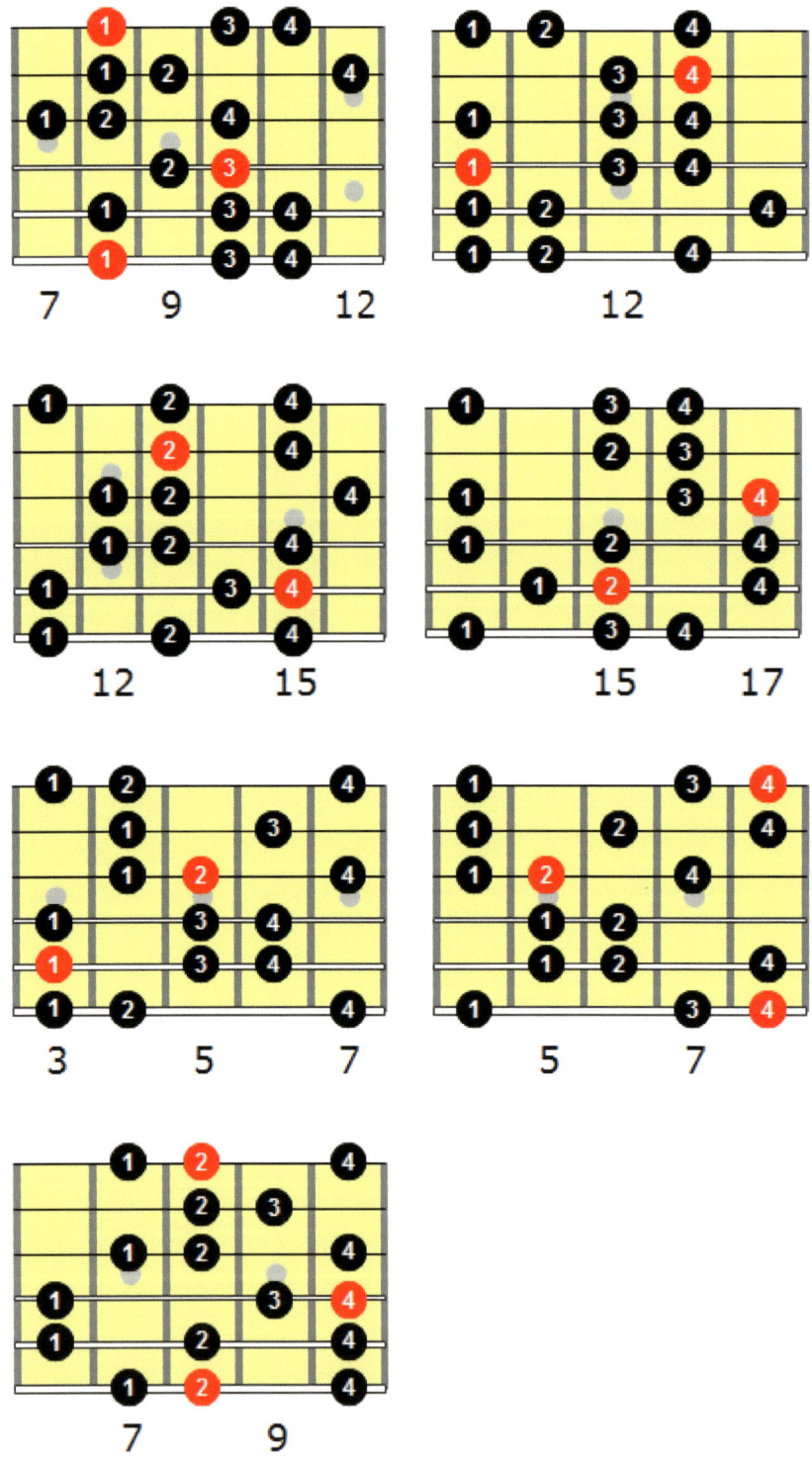

C Harmonic Minor Arpeggios

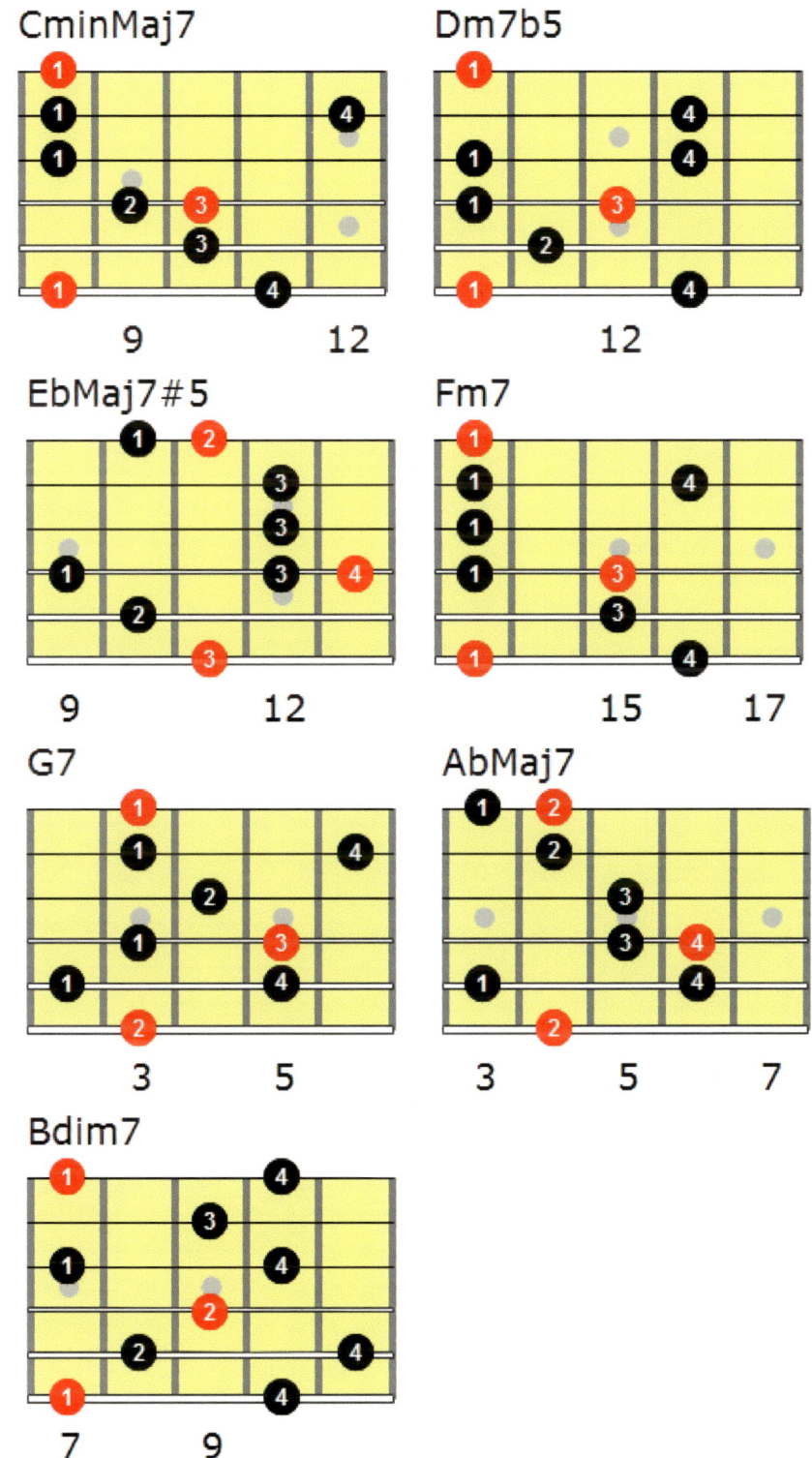

C Hungarian Gypsy Scale

Scale Notes:

C – D – Eb – F# - G – Ab – B - C

Scale Intervals:

W h (W+h) h h (W+h) h

Chords/Arpeggios:

Chord	Spelling
CminMaj7	C – Eb – G – B
D7b5	D – F# - Ab – C
EbMaj7#5	Eb – G – B – D
F#dim7sus4	F# - B – C – Eb
GMaj7	G – B – D – F#
AbMaj7	Ab – C – Eb – G
Bm6	B – D – F# - Ab(G#)

C Hungarian Gypsy Scale Positions

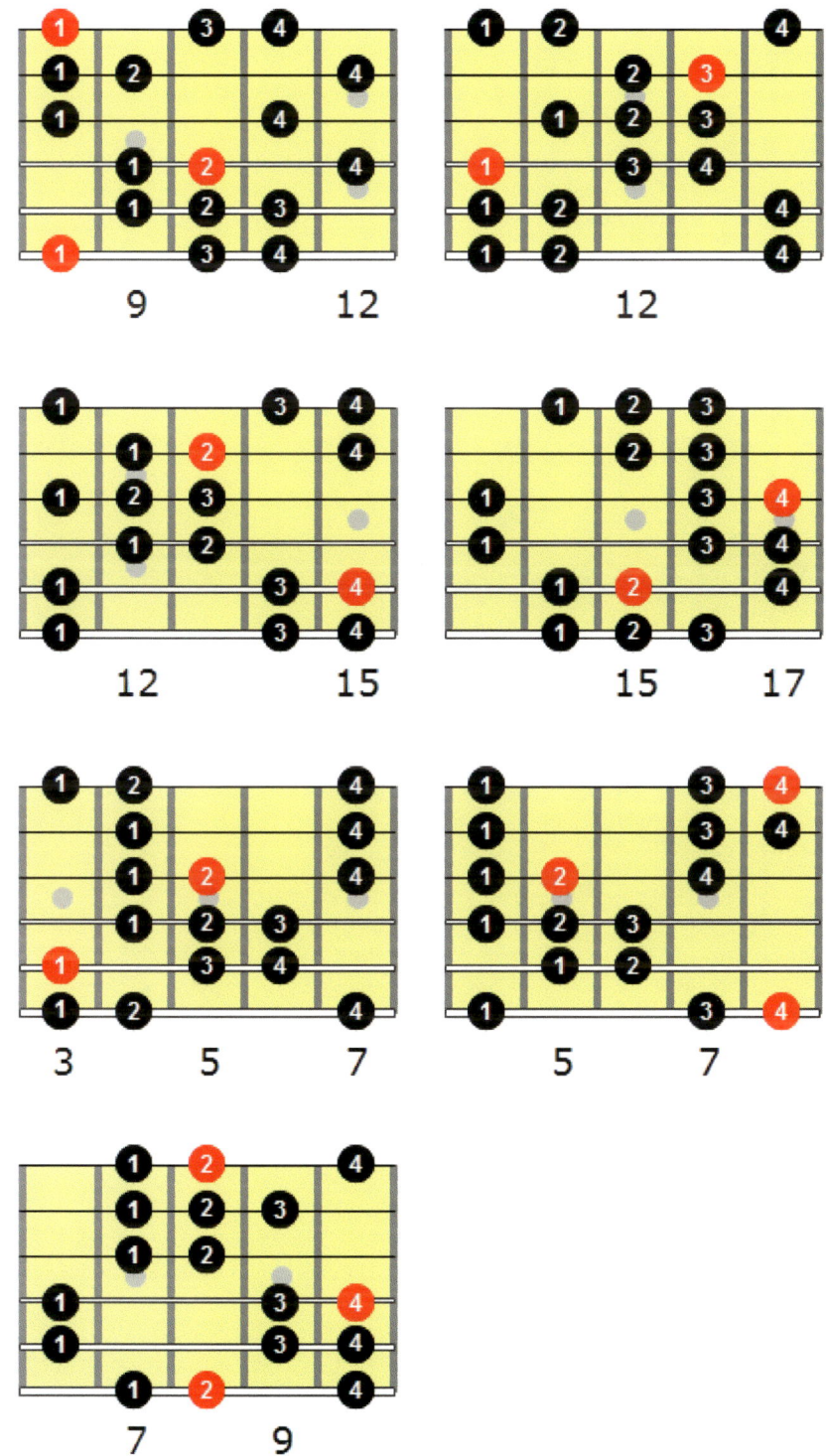

C Hungarian Gypsy Arpeggios

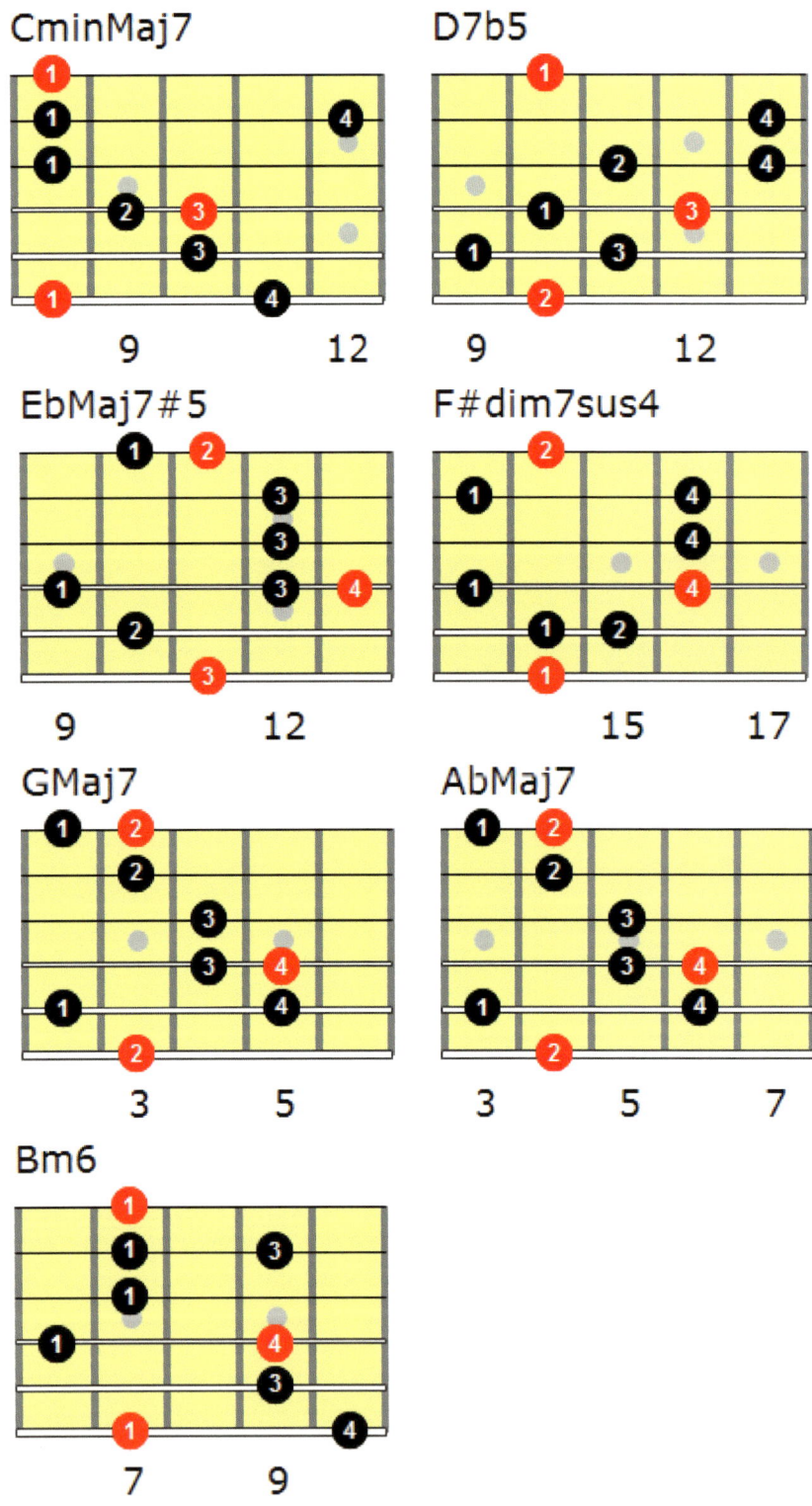

C Japanese (Sakura) Scale

Scale Notes:

C - Db - F - G - Ab - C

Scale Intervals:

h (W+W) W h (W+W)

Chords/Arpeggios:

It's a little difficult to find 7th chords in a Pentatonic scale such as the Japanese scale, but the following are some chords to be found in this scale that make some interesting harmonies and arpeggios:

- C - F - Ab
- Db - F – Ab – C (DbMaj7)
- G – C - Db – F (G7b5sus4)
- Ab – C – F – G (AMaj7add6)

C Japanese (Sakura) Scale Positions

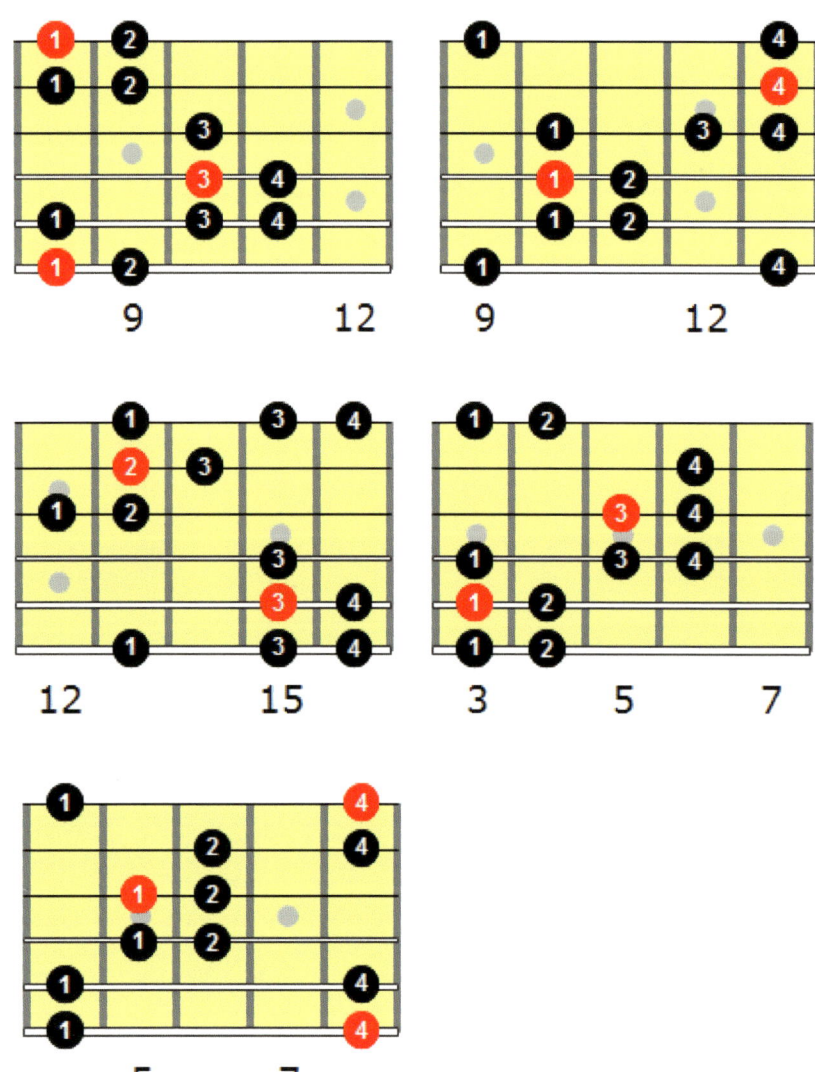

C Japanese (Sakura) Arpeggios

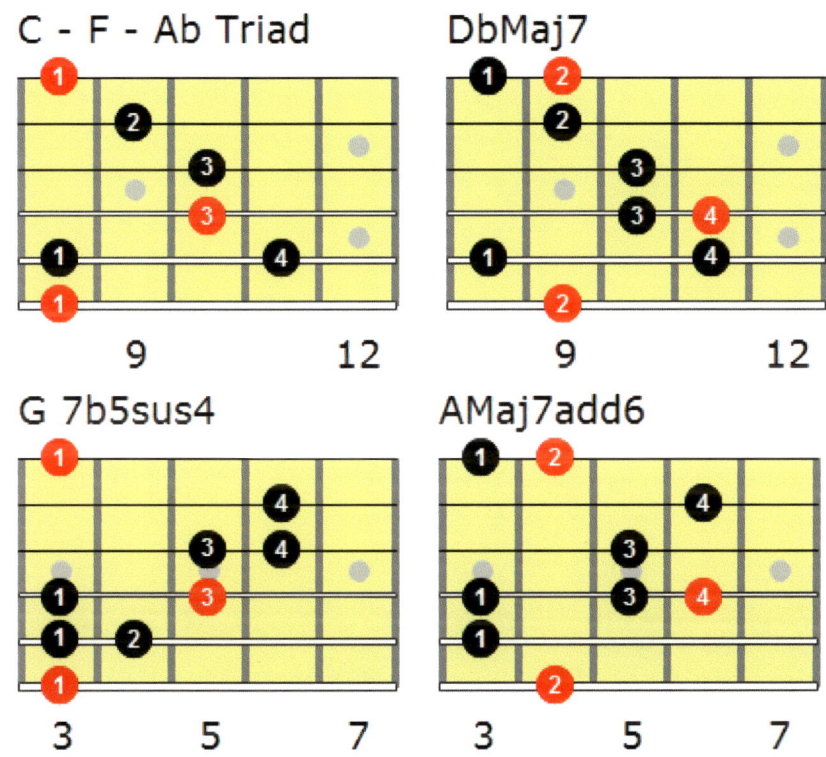

C Neapolitan Major Scale

Scale Notes:

C - Db - Eb - F - G - A - B - C

Scale Intervals:

h W W W W W h

Chords/Arpeggios:

Chord	Spelling
CminMaj7	C - Eb - G - B
Db7#5	Db - F - A – B(Cb)
Eb7#5	Eb - G - B - Db
F7	F - A - C - Eb
G7b5	G - B - Db - F
Amin7b5	A - C - Eb - G
B7b5	B - Eb(D#) - F - A

C Neapolitan Major Scale Positions

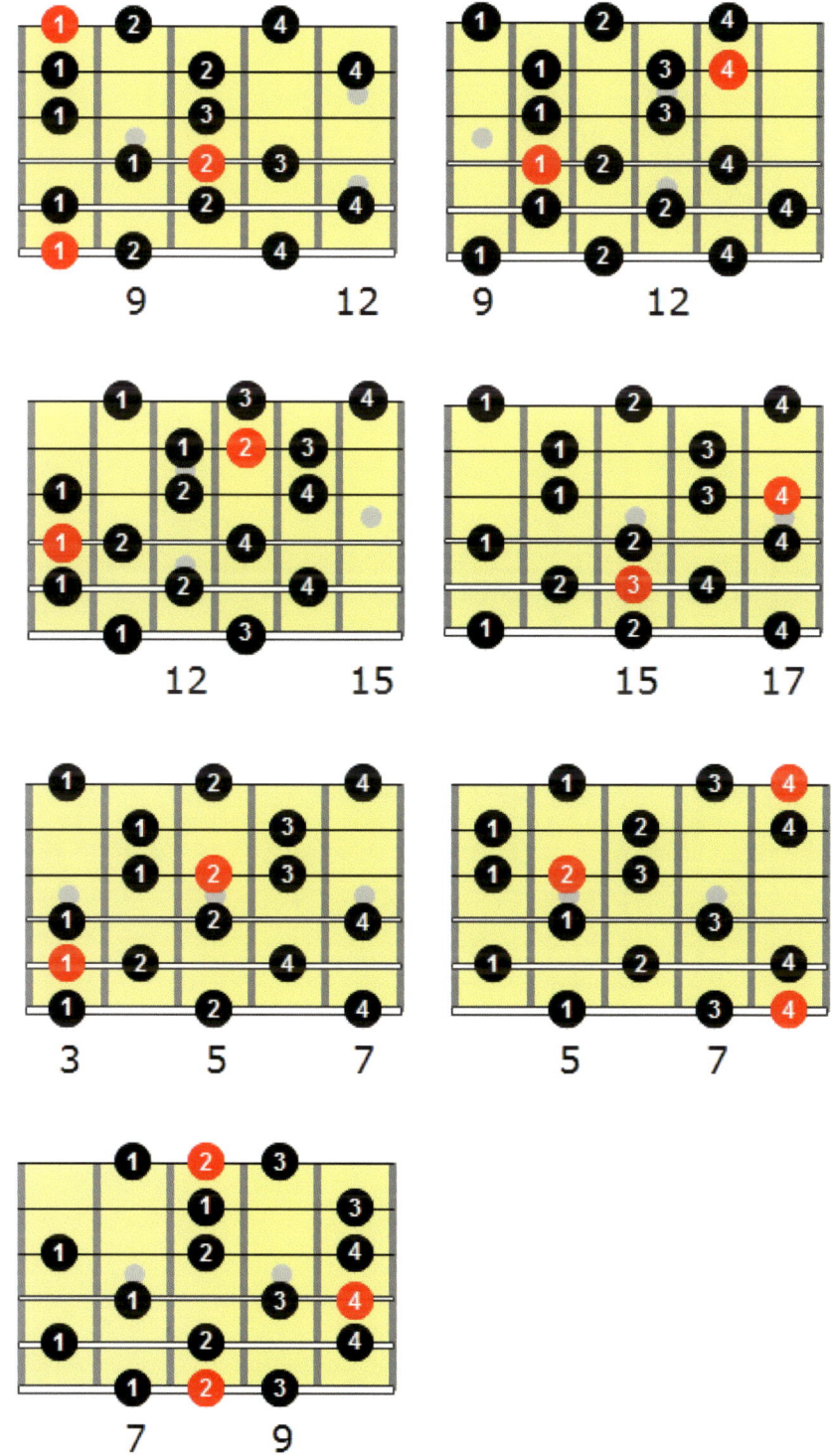

C Neapolitan Major Arpeggios

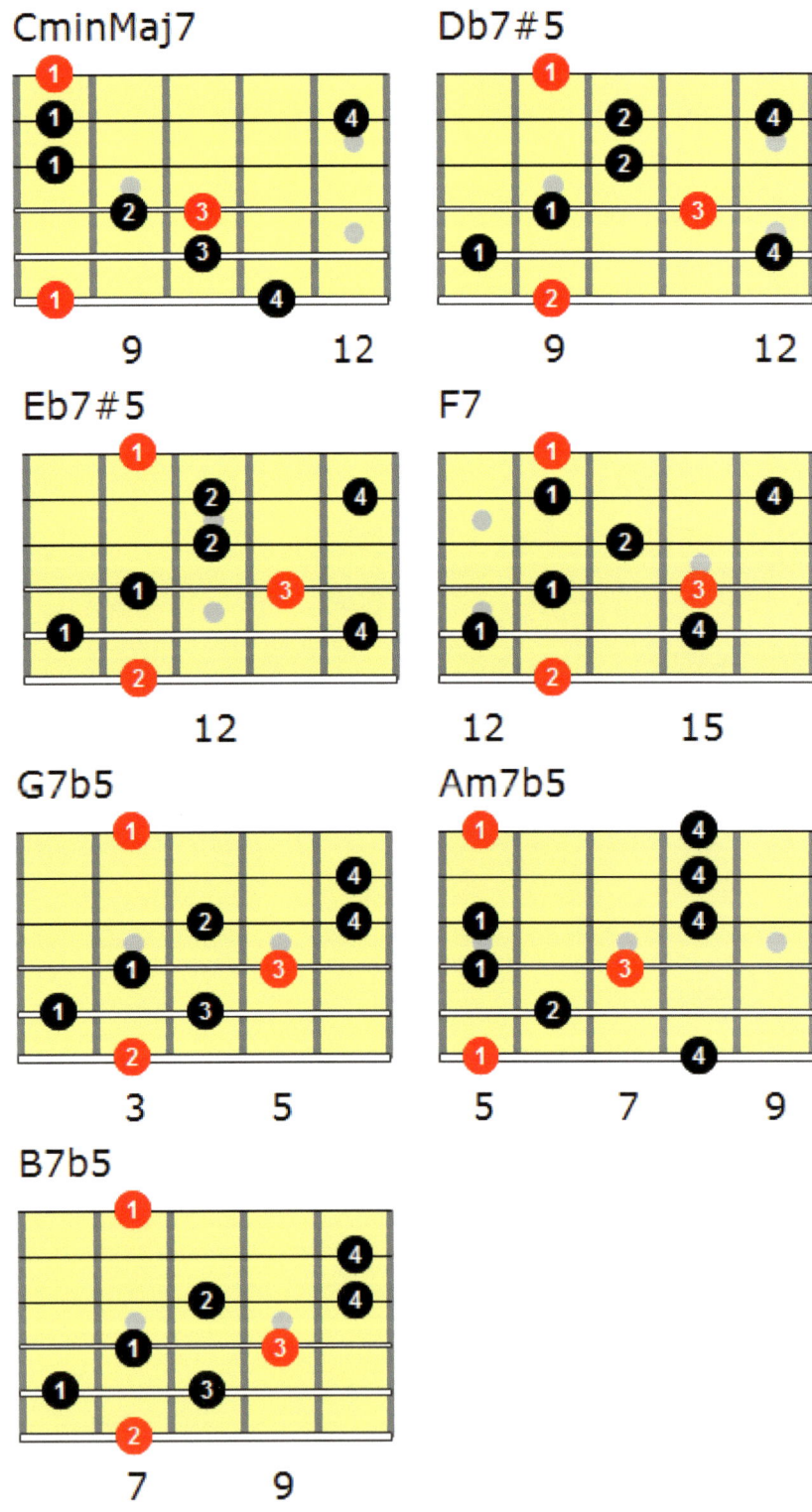

C Neapolitan Minor Scale

Scale Notes:

C - Db - Eb - F - G - Ab - B - C

Scale Intervals:

h W W W h (W+h) h

Chords/Arpeggios:

Chord	Spelling
CminMaj7	C - Eb - G - B
Db7	Db - F - Ab – B(Cb)
Eb7#5	Eb - G - B - Db
Fm7	F - Ab - C - Eb
G7b5	G - B - Db - F
AbMaj7	Ab - C - Eb - G
B6b5	B - Eb(D#) - F - Ab(G#)

C Neapolitan Minor Scale Positions

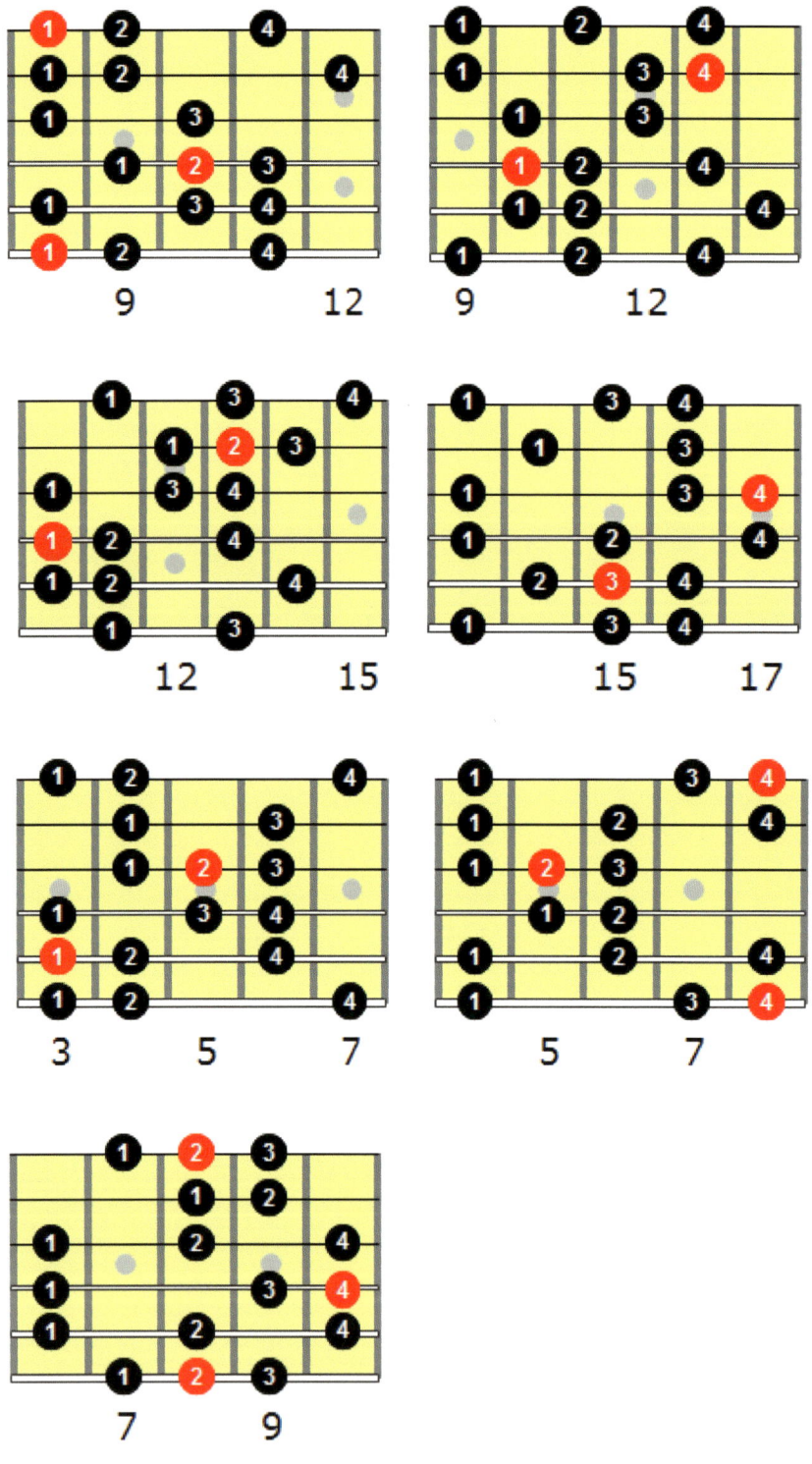

C Neapolitan Minor Arpeggios

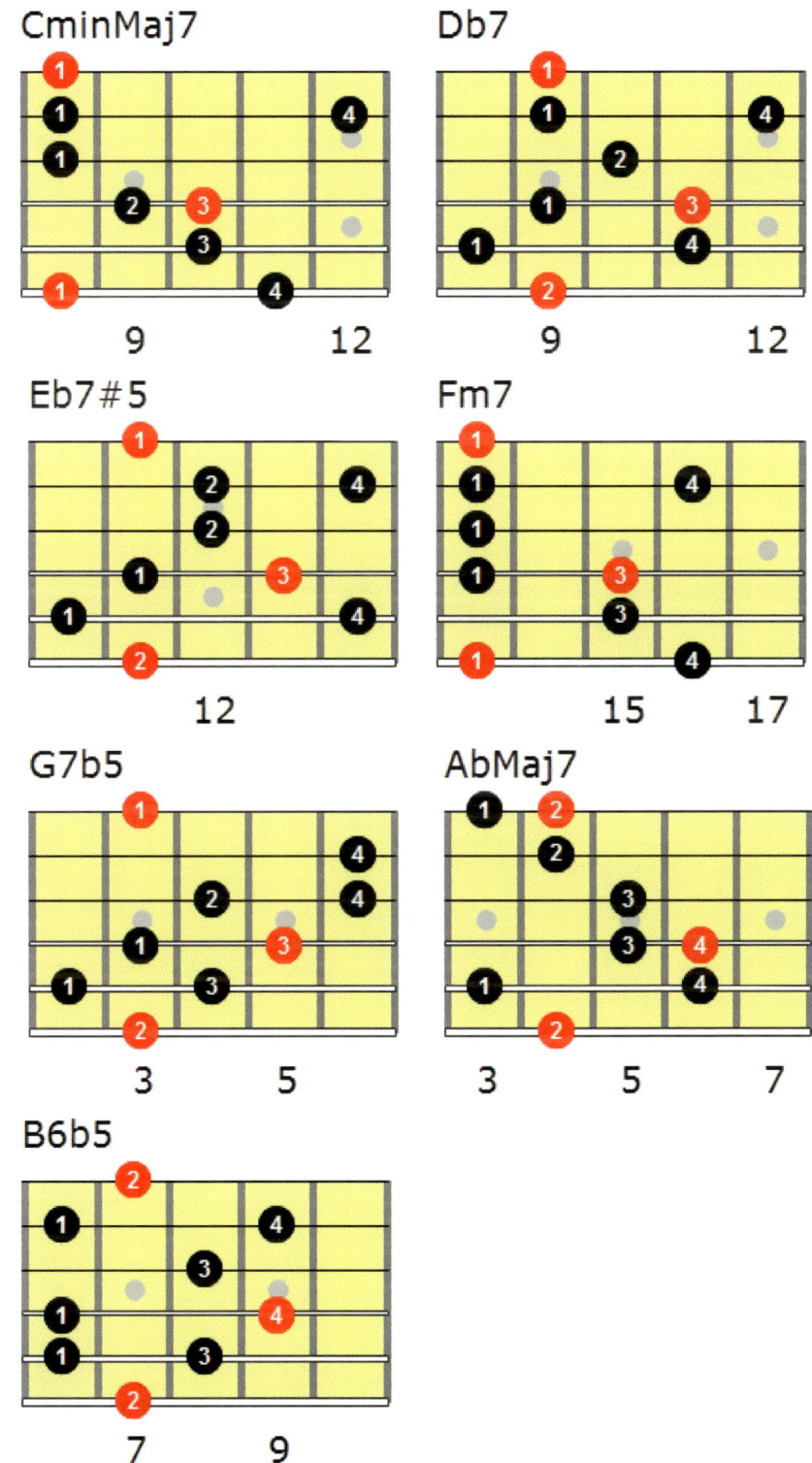

C Persian Scale

Scale Notes:
C - Db - E - F - Gb - Ab - B - C

Scale Intervals:
h (W+h) h h W (W+h) h

Chords/Arpeggios:

Chord	Spelling
CMaj7b5	C - E - Gb - B
Db7	Db - F – Ab – B(Cb)
EMaj6	E - Ab(G#) - B - Db(C#)
FminMaj7	F - Ab - C - E
GbMaj7sus4	Gb - B - Db - F
Ab7#5	Ab - C - E - Gb
Bdim7sus4	B - E - F - Ab

C Persian Scale Positions

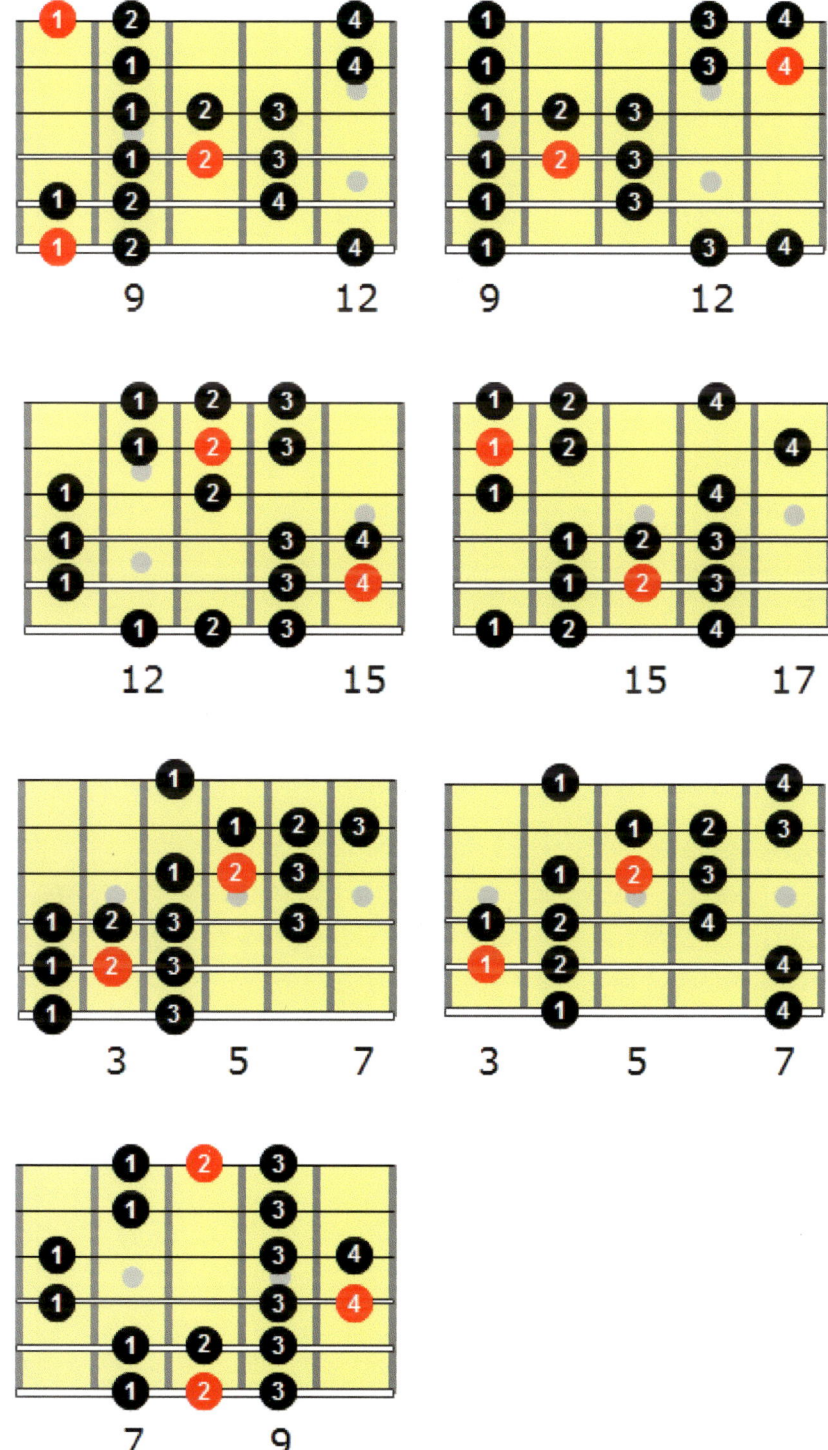

C Persian Scale Arpeggios

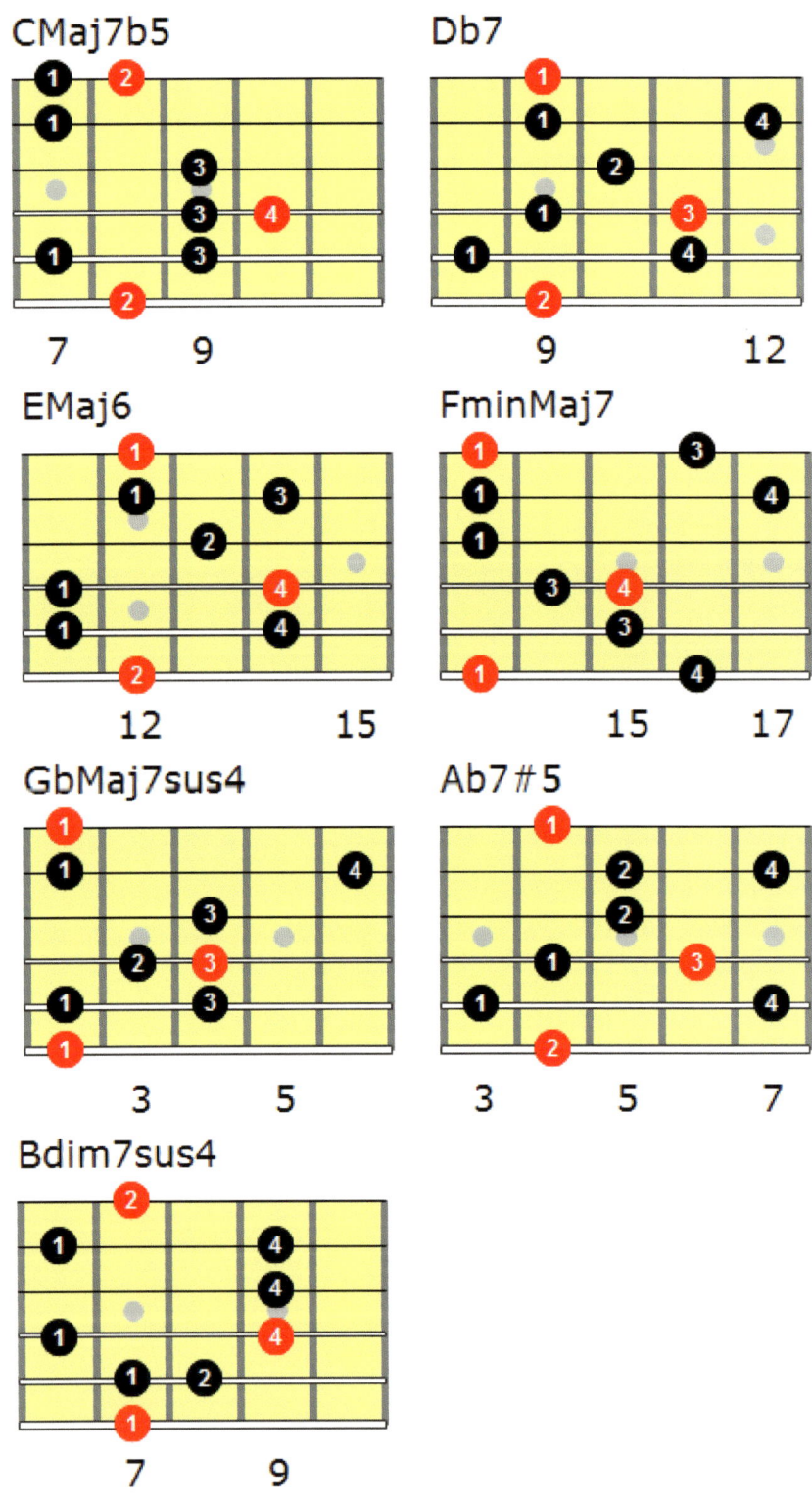

C Prometheus Scale

Scale Notes:

C - D - E - F# - A - Bb - C

Scale Intervals:

W W W (W+h) h W

Chords/Arpeggios:

Chord	Spelling
C7b5	C - E – F#(Gb) - Bb
D7	D - F# - A - C
D7#5	D - F# - Bb(A#) - C
E7b5sus4	E - A - Bb - D
E7+5sus4	E - A - C(B#) - D
F#m7b5	F# - A - C - E
Am6	A - C - E - F#
BbMaj7#5	Bb - D - F# - A

C Prometheus Scale Positions

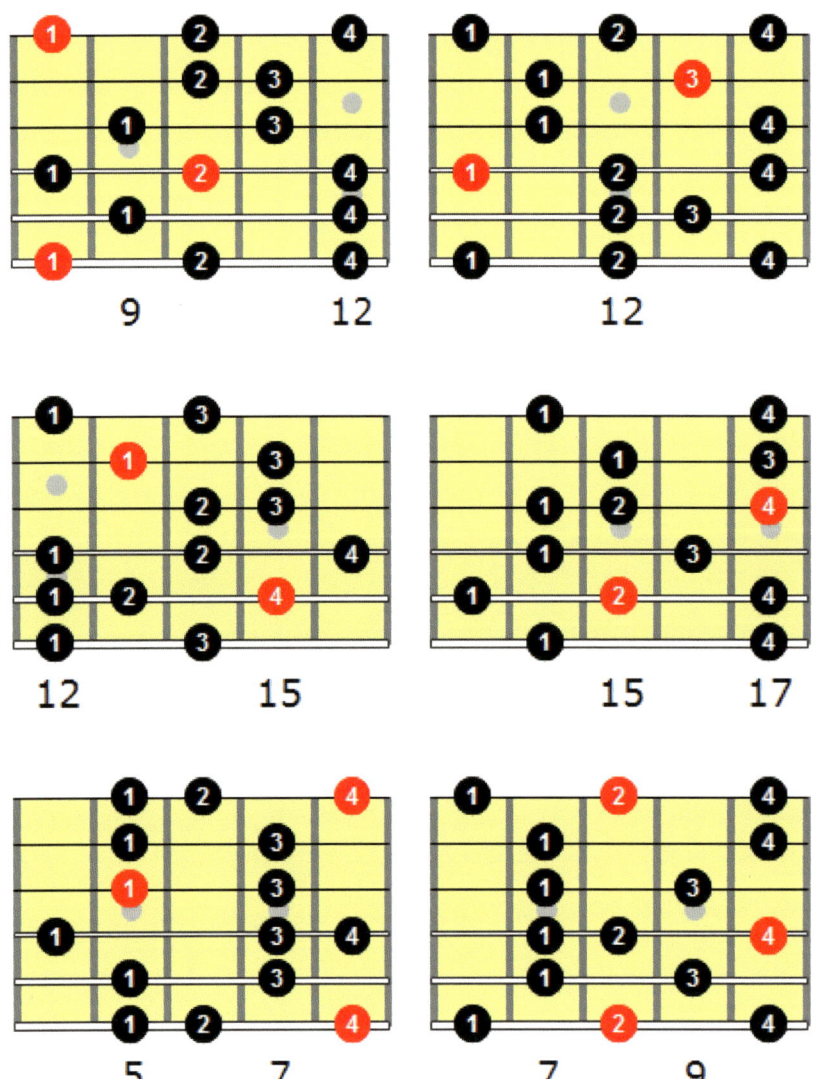

C Prometheus Scale Arpeggios

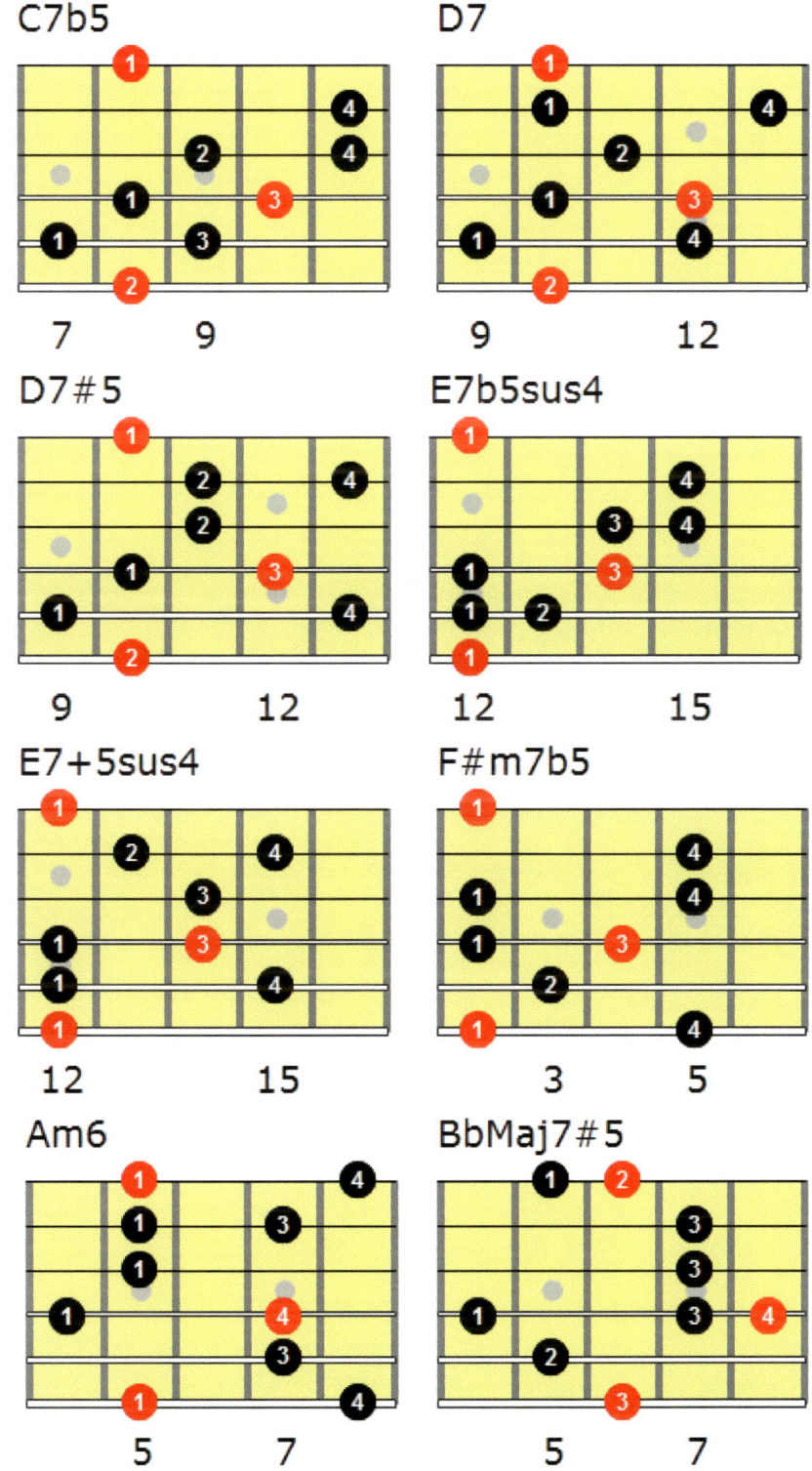

CPSIA information can be obtained at www.ICGtesting.com
Printed in the USA
LVIW01n1253230217
525217LV00004B/21